Save our planet!!

Science Concepts SECOND SERIES

Global Warming

Revised Edition

Alvin Silverstein, Virginia Silverstein,
and Laura Silverstein Nunn

 Twenty-First Century Books

Minneapolis

Twenty-First Century Books
A division of Lerner Publishing Group, Inc.
241 First Avenue North
Minneapolis, MN 55401 U.S.A.

Website address: www.lernerbooks.com

Library of Congress Cataloging-in-Publication Data

Silverstein, Alvin.
    Global warming. — Rev. ed. / by Alvin Silverstein, Virginia Silverstein, Laura Silverstein Nunn.
        p.   cm. — (Science concepts. Second series)
    Includes bibliographical references and index.
    ISBN 978–0–7613–3935–9 (lib. bdg. : alk. paper)
    1. Global warming—Juvenile literature. I. Silverstein, Virginia B. II. Nunn, Laura Silverstein. III. Title.
QC981.8.G56S5494 2009
363.738'74—dc22   2008000409

Manufactured in the United States of America
1 2 3 4 5 6 – DP – 14 13 12 11 10 09

Contents

chapter one

Heating Up

What if you had a remote control that could control

the weather? Would you hit a button to make it warm

and sunny every day? Nonstop sunshine sounds nice,

but rain is important, too. Plants need rain to grow.

Without rain, we wouldn't have anything to eat. And

what about snow? Would you hit the "blizzard" button

from time to time in the winter, so you could have

some days off from school? You could ride your sled

down the hill in the backyard all afternoon or build a

gigantic snowman. Of course there's no such thing

as a weather remote control. We can't control the

weather. Or can we?

A Warming Trend

Many scientists believe that our planet has been on a
warming trend over the last two hundred years. They
say that *our* activities are responsible for this global
warming. It started with the Industrial Revolution,

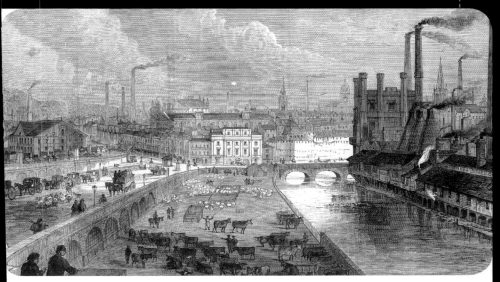

A scene of London, England, shows pollution from smokestacks billowing into the air in the 1800s.

about 1750. At that time, people began to use machines in more areas of life, from heating, to building and manufacturing, to transportation. The machines were powered by burning fuels, such as wood, coal, oil, and natural gas. When these fuels burn, they emit (release) carbon dioxide (CO_2) and other waste products. These chemicals rise into the atmosphere, the layer of air that covers our planet.

Did You Know?

Since the start of the Industrial Revolution, the amount of carbon dioxide in our atmosphere has increased by more than 35 percent!

Carbon dioxide and certain other gases in the atmosphere act like an insulating blanket. They trap heat and hold it close to Earth's surface. Scientists call this the greenhouse effect,

The Greenhouse Effect

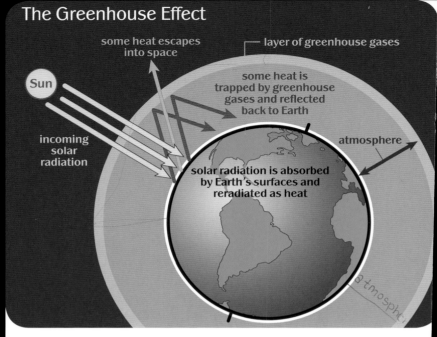

Earth's atmosphere (enlarged in this diagram) acts somewhat like the glass windows and roof of a greenhouse. It lets solar energy reach Earth's surface and then traps some of the escaping heat.

since the gases work in much the same way as the glass windows of a greenhouse, trapping heat inside.

Normally, carbon dioxide is present in the atmosphere in small amounts. There is just enough to keep temperatures on Earth comfortable for our planet's living things. The burning of fuels, however, has been increasing the amount of carbon dioxide in the atmosphere. It's like putting an extra blanket on your bed. The extra carbon dioxide blanket has been making Earth warmer. And warmer temperatures could lead to serious problems for our planet.

Living with Global Warming

So far, global warming has not been very substantial. The average temperature of Earth has increased by a little more than 1°F (0.6°C) in the last one hundred years. This change is so small that some scientists argue that it is just a natural fluctuation and not a trend. Other scientists say there is a great deal of evidence to support global warming: Summers are getting hotter, and winters are getting milder. Glaciers are melting, and sea levels are rising. But these signs are only the start. The warming trend is expected to speed up and produce even greater effects.

Large areas at the North and South poles are covered with ice. But warmer temperatures are already causing that ice to melt. This has contributed to the rising sea levels. If sea levels rise too much, they could flood coastal cities all over the world. The warming may already be affecting the weather in various parts of the planet. We are having more storms, with violent winds and flooding. Eventually, some of today's rich farmlands could become tomorrow's deserts. Other parts of the world, where it has been too cold to grow crops, might become the farmlands of the future. Wildlife species could be forced either to adapt, move, or become extinct, as their habitat changes.

Is it too late to stop global warming? Not necessarily. People and nations all over the world will have to work together to reverse the trend. Simple things, such as planting a tree and recycling your trash, can help. Government regulations and international treaties that limit the emissions of carbon dioxide and other "greenhouse gases" can also slow down or stop global warming. These efforts need to start now, before global warming gets out of control. The longer we wait, the harder it will be to keep conditions just right for life on Earth.

chapter two

Our Planet Earth

From space, Earth looks like a giant marble with swirls of blue, green, brown, and white. The white clouds that surround our planet are made of water vapor. Water vapor comes from the surface of oceans, lakes, and rivers. Some of the surface water evaporates, turning from a liquid into a gas. When the clouds condense, they produce rain, snow, sleet, and hail. In this way, they return water to the surface. This process, called the water cycle, is one of the most important cycles on our planet. This is nature's way of recycling water.

Earth is the only planet in our solar system that has both liquid water and solid ice. Conditions can vary greatly on Earth. Our planet has icy poles; hot, dry deserts; swampy rain forests; and temperate regions with a mild climate. Millions of different kinds of animals and plants have found homes and ways to survive in the varied habitats that the lands and waters provide. Life can be found just about anywhere on Earth's surface because temperatures do not get too hot or too cold for living things to survive.

Earth's Atmosphere

Life would not be possible without Earth's atmosphere. The insulating blanket that surrounds our planet stretches about 600 miles (966 kilometers) into space. It is thickest close to the surface, where the pull of Earth's gravity is strongest.

The white clouds that surround Earth are visible in this National Aeronautics and Space Administration (NASA) image.

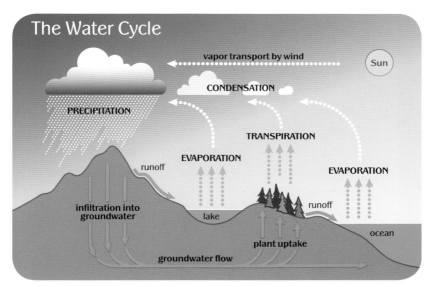

Nature recycles water between the lands and the seas of Earth's surface and the water vapor in the atmosphere. Evaporation and precipitation are important parts of the cycle. Plants and animals also play a major role.

(Gravity is a force that attracts objects to Earth. It keeps the atmosphere from floating off into space.) We call the part of the atmosphere closest to the surface "air." This layer of the atmosphere, about 6 to 10 miles (10 to 16 km) thick, is a mixture of gases: about four-fifths nitrogen and the rest mostly oxygen. It also has small amounts of water vapor, carbon dioxide, and several other gases.

What's in the Air?

Gas	Amount
Nitrogen	78 percent
Oxygen	21 percent
Argon	0.9 percent
Carbon dioxide	0.03 percent
Water vapor	varying amounts
Hydrogen	traces
Ozone	traces
Methane	traces
Carbon monoxide	traces
Helium	traces
Neon	traces
Krypton	traces
Xenon	traces

Nearly all living things take in oxygen from the air or water and use it to get stored energy out of food. This energy powers all of their activities. They could not live without it. The oxygen that animals breathe in combines with food materials in a chemical reaction. It is a sort of "burning" that releases the energy stored inside them. Carbon dioxide is produced as a by-product, which is then sent into the atmosphere.

The sun's radiations that reach Earth contain not only the light we can see but also ultraviolet (UV) radiation. UV rays can cause harmful effects ranging from sunburn to cancer. But the atmosphere acts as a protective shield, screening out most of the harmful radiations.

Our blanket of air also helps to distribute heat from the sun's radiations more evenly over Earth's surface. While half of the planet is turned toward the sun, the other half is in darkness. Earth rotates, or turns, so that each spot on the surface receives sunlight for at least part of the day. The lands and the oceans absorb heat while the sun is shining, so they remain warm for some time after the sun sets. The oceans actually hold more heat than the lands, and they store it for a longer time. Gases in the atmosphere, such as carbon dioxide, also absorb heat and send it back to Earth's surface.

Nature Recycles

We've already seen how Earth recycles water, which is continually exchanged between the atmosphere and the planet's surface. Other key chemicals are also recycled by natural processes, such as the nitrogen cycle, the oxygen cycle, and the carbon cycle.

What a Difference an Atmosphere Makes

What would Earth be like without an atmosphere? To get some idea, take a look at the moon. Both Earth and the moon are about the same distance from the sun and receive the same amount of energy, averaged over a year's time. But the moon doesn't have an atmosphere, so its average surface temperature is -0.4°F (-18°C), while Earth's is 59°F (15°C). Our planet is much warmer than its moon because its atmosphere traps heat energy and keeps it from escaping into space.

The surface of the moon as seen from the Galileo space probe. Without an atmosphere to trap heat, the moon is mu colder than Earth.

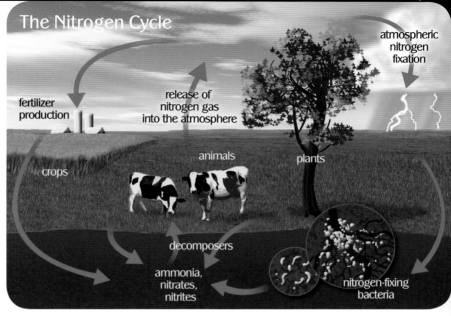

The Nitrogen Cycle

atmospheric nitrogen fixation

fertilizer production

release of nitrogen gas into the atmosphere

animals

plants

crops

decomposers

ammonia, nitrates, nitrites

nitrogen-fixing bacteria

Animals, plants, and bacteria all contribute to nature's recycling of nitrogen. Nitrogen gas in the atmosphere is converted to forms that living things can use. It is then returned to the atmosphere when wastes and dead matter decompose.

Some of the nitrogen in the atmosphere is changed into other chemical forms by bacteria that live in the soil. Plants take up nitrates and other nitrogen chemicals from the soil and use them in building proteins and other important compounds. Animals get nitrogen for their own body chemicals by eating plants. When plants and animals die, their bodies decay, returning nitrogen compounds to the soil. These compounds are eventually broken down to nitrogen gas that is returned to the atmosphere.

Oxygen is an important element for life. Animals take oxygen out of the air when they breathe, and they release carbon dioxide into the atmosphere. Plants breathe, too, but they take in far more carbon dioxide than they produce.

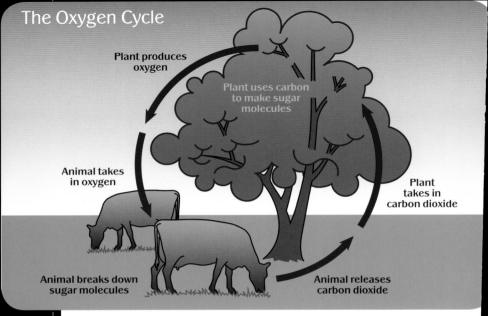

The Oxygen Cycle

Plant produces oxygen

Plant uses carbon to make sugar molecules

Animal takes in oxygen

Plant takes in carbon dioxide

Animal breaks down sugar molecules

Animal releases carbon dioxide

Both animals and plants need to take in oxygen, but the amount of this gas in the atmosphere stays the same because of nature's recycling processes. Photosynthesis replaces the oxygen that living things use up.

In a process called photosynthesis, plants use the sun's energy to turn water, carbon dioxide, and other raw materials into food. Oxygen is released as a by-product. Animals that eat plants also use the food materials that plants make, benefiting indirectly from the stored sunlight energy. The amounts of oxygen that enter and leave the atmosphere are in balance so that the total amount of oxygen in the atmosphere stays the same.

The burning of fuels—in the furnaces that heat our homes and power our factories, the stoves that cook our food, and the engines that run our cars—also uses oxygen from the atmosphere, converting it to carbon dioxide. This part of the cycle has been increasing steadily as the world becomes more industrialized. However, Earth's plants give off far more oxygen during photosynthesis than the amount used up by burning fuels. So the increased use of oxygen for human activities has not been enough to upset the oxygen balance.

The oxygen cycle is interlinked with the carbon cycle. Carbon is a basic element found in every living thing on Earth. It can be built into a number of different complex chemicals, such as proteins, sugars, and fats. This element is also a major part of fossil fuels: coal, oil, and natural gas. These are the remains of dead plants and animals, which were buried in the mud millions of years ago. They were "cooked" by the enormous temperatures and pressures deep below the surface. The connecting link between the carbon and oxygen cycles is carbon dioxide. When food materials are broken down in a body or when fuels are burned in a fire, the carbon that they contain combines with oxygen to form carbon dioxide.

Plants take in carbon dioxide from the air and use it to make food materials by photosynthesis. Thus, the plants on land and the plantlike organisms in the oceans remove huge amounts of carbon dioxide from the atmosphere. Scientists say that plants are an important carbon dioxide "sink."

Rain also takes carbon dioxide out of the atmosphere (the gas dissolves in water). The rain carries it to streams and rivers and ultimately to the oceans. Carbon dioxide may also dissolve directly into the surface waters of lakes and oceans. These bodies of water are also important carbon dioxide sinks. Earth's oceans contain sixty times as much carbon dioxide as there is in the atmosphere.

The carbon in the bodies of phytoplankton, plantlike organisms that live on the ocean surface, is removed from the cycle when they die and sink to the ocean bottom. But the carbon in land plants and animals is recycled when they die and their bodies decay. So they take carbon out of the atmosphere only *temporarily*. Carbon compounds in rocks may

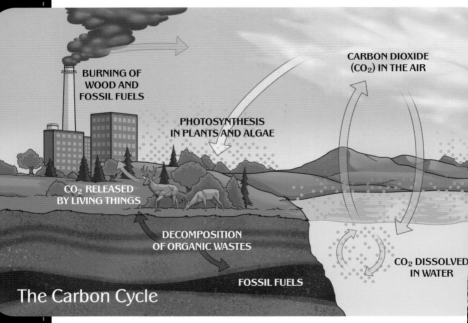

BURNING OF
WOOD AND
FOSSIL FUELS

CARBON DIOXIDE
(CO_2) IN THE AIR

PHOTOSYNTHESIS
IN PLANTS AND ALGAE

CO_2 RELEASED
BY LIVING THINGS

DECOMPOSITION
OF ORGANIC WASTES

CO_2 DISSOLVED
IN WATER

FOSSIL FUELS

The Carbon Cycle

Nature recycles carbon in many ways. Living things, decomposing material, and the burning of fuels all release carbon dioxide. Plants and algae take in carbon dioxide from air and water. The ocean absorbs some atmospheric carbon dioxide. It also releases carbon dioxide back into the air.

also be returned to the cycle when they are dissolved in rainwater or vaporized by erupting volcanoes.

Though the increased burning of fuels has not upset the balance of the oxygen cycle, it is having a much greater effect on the carbon cycle. People are generating more carbon dioxide than the oceans and plants can soak up. As a result, the amount of this gas in the atmosphere is increasing. Remember, oxygen makes up nearly 21 percent of the atmosphere, but air contains only about 0.03 percent carbon dioxide. So a small change in the amount of oxygen would have almost no effect on the oxygen balance. But a similar change in the amount of carbon dioxide can greatly upset the balance in the carbon cycle. That's why scientists are worried about the buildup of carbon dioxide in the atmosphere and the effects it may have on our planet.

chapter three

The Greenhouse Effect

Global warming has been making headlines lately, but it is not a new idea. The greenhouse effect was first described in 1827 by French scientist Jean-Baptiste Fourier, who compared Earth's atmosphere to the glass of a greenhouse. Fourier suggested that this effect was keeping Earth warmer than it would be otherwise.

Irish scientist John Tyndall published a paper in 1863 reporting that water vapor in the atmosphere is a heat-trapping gas involved in the greenhouse effect. In the 1890s, a Swedish scientist, Svante Arrhenius, and an American, P. C. Chamberlain, both suggested that a buildup of carbon dioxide in the air could cause problems for the planet. They believed that the widespread burning of coal and other fuels could lead to global warming.

How the Greenhouse Effect Works

Although it's called the greenhouse effect, the process does not really involve trapping heat in exactly the same way a greenhouse does. Most greenhouses look like small houses with glass roofs and walls. As sunlight passes through the glass panes, it is absorbed by everything in the greenhouse, including the plants. As the plants and soil get heated, they generate a form of energy called infrared radiation (heat energy). Infrared radiation flows out toward the glass panes, but it cannot pass through glass as light can. So the heat energy becomes trapped. And the greenhouse heats up. (The same thing happens inside a car parked in sunlight.) This trapped heat keeps the plants warm enough to live and grow through the cold winter.

Like the glass in a greenhouse, Earth's atmosphere allows the sun's light energy to pass through. As sunlight showers over Earth, it is absorbed by plants, the ground, the ocean, and everything else on the planet. These things produce

These poinsettia plants grow in a greenhouse. Earth's atmosphere works like the glass in a greenhouse, letting in the sun's energy but trapping gases and heat energy.

infrared radiation and radiate it back toward space. Some of the radiation manages to escape into space. But some of it becomes trapped when it is absorbed by the gases in the atmosphere. The radiation in the atmosphere is then sent back to Earth's surface. The more radiation trapped in the atmosphere, the warmer our planet becomes.

That's where the similarities between a greenhouse and the greenhouse effect end. The big difference is that there is no movement of air in a greenhouse, so the temperatures are continually warm. The only way you can control the temperature inside a greenhouse is to open or close the ventilators in its roof. Temperatures on our planet would be constant too, if it were not for the movements of air in our atmosphere. Earth's surface can lose heat as a result of rising warm air currents and falling cold air currents. It can also lose heat when water on the ocean surface evaporates and returns to the atmosphere in the form of water vapor. This gas may later condense into rain or snow.

The gases involved in the greenhouse effect are commonly called greenhouse gases. They include carbon dioxide, water vapor, methane, nitrous oxide, chlorofluorocarbons (CFCs), and ozone.

The Real No. 1 Greenhouse Gas

Water vapor is actually the most important greenhouse gas. The amounts of water vapor in the atmosphere are greater than those of carbon dioxide, methane, or any other heat-trapping gases. Water vapor accounts for an estimated 60 to 70 percent of the greenhouse effect. However, it occurs naturally in the atmosphere and is not due to human activities.

Unlike other greenhouse gases, water vapor doesn't stay in the atmosphere very long. It returns to the surface as rain or snow within a week or so. The amount of water vapor in the atmosphere—the humidity—depends on the weather, the location, and the time of year. Temperature also has a big effect: Warm air can hold more water vapor. So as Earth's temperature rises, the contribution of the No. 1 greenhouse gas increases.

The Carbon Dioxide Problem

We add more carbon dioxide to the atmosphere than any other gas. Scientists believe that this greenhouse gas accounts for about 55 percent of the global warming due to human activities.

You can see carbon dioxide at work by taking a look at the planet Venus. You would expect Venus to be somewhat warmer than Earth since it is closer to the sun. But it is a *lot* warmer—a sizzling 900°F (482°C) both day and night! That's because Venus's atmosphere is a much better heat trap.

Greenhouse Gases

Contribution to greenhouse gases:

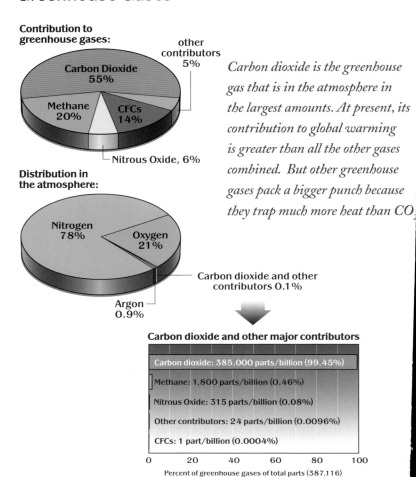

Carbon dioxide is the greenhouse gas that is in the atmosphere in the largest amounts. At present, its contribution to global warming is greater than all the other gases combined. But other greenhouse gases pack a bigger punch because they trap much more heat than CO_2.

Carbon Dioxide 55%

Methane 20%

CFCs 14%

other contributors 5%

Nitrous Oxide, 6%

Distribution in the atmosphere:

Nitrogen 78%

Oxygen 21%

Argon 0.9%

Carbon dioxide and other contributors 0.1%

Carbon dioxide and other major contributors

Carbon dioxide: 385,000 parts/billion (99.45%)

Methane: 1,800 parts/billion (0.46%)

Nitrous Oxide: 315 parts/billion (0.08%)

Other contributors: 24 parts/billion (0.0096%)

CFCs: 1 part/billion (0.0004%)

| 0 | 20 | 40 | 60 | 80 | 100 |

Percent of greenhouse gases of total parts (387,116)

Earth's environment is so delicately balanced that tiny changes can have huge effects. If we manage to cut the amounts of CO_2 released into the atmosphere, but those of other greenhouse gases such as methane and nitrous oxide continue to rise, their contributions may someday outweigh the warming effect of carbon dioxide.

It contains 95 percent carbon dioxide. That's more more than ten thousand times as much carbon dioxide as in Earth's atmosphere.

Scientists used to think that the amount of carbon dioxide in Earth's atmosphere would stay the same. They assumed that the excess carbon dioxide produced by human activities would dissolve in the oceans. Or it would be used for photosynthesis by the plantlife on the land and in the oceans. The amount of carbon dioxide that these sinks can hold has been decreasing, however. Pollution in oceans and lakes, for example, kills large amounts of phytoplankton. Normally, about three-quarters of the photosynthesis on our planet occurs in the oceans.

At the same time, people are cutting down trees to make way for more buildings, roads, farms, and parking lots. They also use the wood for building materials, pulp for paper manufacture, and fuel. But deforestation—clearing the land of vegetation—*reduces* the amount of photosynthesis. New trees may be planted to replace the ones that were cut down. But the seedlings are much smaller with far less leaf area for photosynthesis. As a result, carbon dioxide builds up in the atmosphere because fewer carbon dioxide sinks are available to remove it.

Deforestation can also add extra carbon dioxide to the atmosphere. In some parts of the world, especially the tropics, forests are burned to clear land for farming. In "slash and burn" agriculture, for example, farmers cut down a few acres of trees and burn the tree trunks. There is an added benefit. The ash that is left enriches the soil and helps to give a rich yield of crops. This benefit is only temporary, however. Without the tree roots to hold water in the soil, rain soon washes away ash minerals. After a few years, the farmers move on to clear more forest. Meanwhile, burning forests releases carbon dioxide gas.

Shrinking Forests

Worldwide, about 10 billion acres (4 billion hectares) are covered with forests. That's about 30 percent of the total land area. But from 1990 to 2005, 3 percent of the world's forests were destroyed. The loss was greatest in developing countries. Industrialized nations actually increased their total forest areas, but many old-growth forests, which had been around for thousands of years, were lost. Old-growth forests contain the largest numbers of animal and plant species.

Fires burn in the Amazon rain forest in South America as land is cleared for cattle grazing. The fires pour carbon dioxide into the atmosphere and destroy plants that could soak up this greenhouse gas.

In 2007 researchers from the Global Carbon Project reported that since 2000, the amount of carbon dioxide in the atmosphere has been increasing 35 percent faster than expected. Nearly half of this increase could be explained by increased burning of fossil fuels. But the rest of the increase seems to be due to the fact that Earth's natural sinks, such as plant life and oceans, are not removing as much carbon dioxide from the atmosphere as they did before. The Southern Ocean around Antarctica, in particular, has become windier as a result of global warming. Churning winds lead to a release of carbon dioxide that had been stored deep in the ocean, and they prevent the water from absorbing more greenhouse gases.

What About Methane?

Methane produced by human activities is the second most important greenhouse gas. It traps twenty-five times more heat than carbon dioxide, but the amounts of methane in the atmosphere are far smaller. (As of 2007, the carbon dioxide concentration in the atmosphere was about 385 parts per million—that is, 385 molecules of CO_2 for every one million molecules of air. The methane concentration was 1,800 parts per *billion*—that is, less than two methane molecules per million air molecules.) Scientists estimate that methane accounts for about 20 percent of human-related global warming.

Some of the methane in the atmosphere is formed naturally. It is sometimes called swamp gas because it is generated by bacteria found in wet environments, such as swamps and rice paddies. Methane also enters the atmosphere when bacteria break down organic material in landfills, garbage

Above: *Cows graze in a field. As cows digest food, they burp up methane gas. Their waste is also a source of nitrous oxide.*
Below: *Landfills and garbage dumps are sources of methane, as bacteria break down materials.*

dumps, and sewage treatment facilities.

Farm animals are another major source of methane in the atmosphere. Bacteria that live in the guts of cows help to digest their food. Up to 10 percent of this food is turned into methane gas. So every time a cow burps or passes gas, it releases methane into the air. Sheep, goats, buffalo, and camels burp out methane, too. As human populations continue to grow, so does the demand for meat and dairy products. The number of cattle has doubled since the 1960s. And more cattle means more methane trapping heat in the atmosphere.

Drilling for oil and natural gas also sends methane into the atmosphere. Natural gas is mostly methane, which can escape during leaks, drilling, production, or transportation. This gas also escapes during coal mining.

In 2007 the amount of methane in the atmosphere suddenly increased sharply, after remaining fairly constant for a decade. Part of the increase probably resulted from increases in meat consumption (more cattle, more burps) and coal mining. But scientists believe that the methane level is also rising because of global warming. Wetlands in the tropics are sending out more methane. In the Arctic region, lands that had remained frozen for centuries are starting to thaw. The layer of frozen soil, called permafrost, holds enormous

A scientist measures the ground-level temperature in Arctic northern Alaska. Recent ground-level warming is melting permafrost across vast areas of Arctic Alaska.

amounts of trapped methane. When the permafrost thaws, this methane passes into the atmosphere. The larger amounts of this powerful greenhouse gas may speed up global warming, leading to more thawing of frozen soil and more methane release.

Other Greenhouse Gases

The third in the list of human-generated greenhouse gases is nitrous oxide. It's a powerful one, trapping heat 310 times more effectively than carbon dioxide. Nitrous oxide occurs naturally in the environment. It is released from oceans and by bacteria in the soil. It is also generated by car exhausts and factory smokestacks. A major source of nitrous oxide is nitrogen-based fertilizer used by farmers to enrich the soil so they can grow more crops. Homeowners also spread fertilizer on their lawns to make the grass grow faster. Scientists believe that nitrous oxide is responsible for about 6 percent of the warming due to human-generated greenhouse gases.

Chlorofluorocarbons (CFCs) are the most powerful human-generated greenhouse gases. They trap heat 10,000 times more effectively than carbon dioxide! CFCs do not occur naturally in the environment. They are human-made gases. CFCs and other fluorocarbons account for about 14 percent of the warming due to human-generated greenhouse gases.

For years, CFCs were used as coolants in freezers, refrigerators, and air conditioners. In the 1970s, scientists discovered that these powerful chemicals were destroying ozone in the upper atmosphere, forming an "ozone hole." Ozone is a gas that is formed by the action of the sun's ultraviolet radiation on oxygen molecules. It normally acts as a shield, protecting us from the sun's harmful radiation. Since the ozone hole first formed, more UV radiation has been reaching Earth's surface. UV rays can lead to skin cancer and other health problems. By 1998, 160 countries had agreed to stop using CFCs. CFCs have been replaced with hydrofluorocarbons (HFCs). HFCs do not harm the ozone layer, but they do contribute to global warming.

The Other Ozone

The thinning of the ozone layer in the upper atmosphere really has nothing to do with global warming. Ozone in the lower atmosphere, however, is a greenhouse gas. It forms when lightning passes through the oxygen in the atmosphere. But more often it is produced by factories and automobiles. This ozone can pollute the air. It contributes to smog and can be a health hazard, causing breathing difficulties.

chapter four

Our Changing Climate

When scientists talk about global warming, they're not exactly talking about the weather. Actually, they are more interested in the world's climate. People often confuse weather and climate, but they are not the same thing. Weather is the condition of the atmosphere from one day to the next. Today is sunny and warm; yesterday was rainy and cool. Climate, on the other hand, is determined on a more long-term basis. Climate is a pattern of weather conditions for a particular place over a long period of time.

Climatologists, scientists who study climate, find out the climate of a region by studying it over a period of years. Climate is determined according to average monthly and yearly temperatures and amounts of precipitation. Phoenix, Arizona, for example, has a warm, dry climate. Fairbanks, Alaska, is cold much of the year, with plenty of ice and snow. Climatologists also consider how seasons vary throughout the year.

A stream of meltwater runs off part of Greenland's ice sheet. Rising temperatures are rapidly melting Greenland's ice.

Climatologists say that our planet's average climate is changing to warmer temperatures around the world. Yet Earth has already gone through a number of climatic changes.

Climate through the Ages

In much of the United States, the climate seems predictable. Summers are warm, and winters are cold. Over the ages, however, our planet has alternated between periods of warm

Extent of Glaciers in Last Ice Age

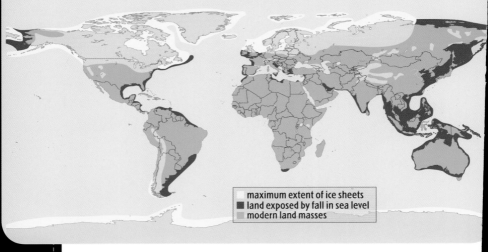

maximum extent of ice sheets
land exposed by fall in sea level
modern land masses

About one hundred ten thousand years ago, a cooling of Earth's surface led to global climate change. Huge sheets of glacial ice covered large parts of several continents, reaching maximum coverage about eighteen thousand years ago. So much water froze that the sea level fell along many coastlines.

weather and periods of cold weather. The coldest temperatures on Earth occurred during the ice ages. They mark the most dramatic changes in Earth's climate. During an ice age, large sheets of ice, called glaciers, cover the lands in certain parts of the world.

Ice ages have been occurring on our planet at regular intervals for the past two million years. The last ice age ended about ten thousand years ago. During that time, glaciers covered all of Canada, much of the United States, and most of northwestern Europe. The ice was hundreds and even thousands of feet thick. Today glaciers cover about 10 percent of Earth's land area and contain about 75 percent of all the freshwater on our planet.

In between each ice age are periods of warming called interglacial periods. (The term *glacial* is often used to describe an ice age. Therefore, the term *interglacial* means "between ice ages.") During these times, snow and ice melt, and glaciers retreat—covering a smaller land area. We have been in an interglacial period since the last ice age. The only remains of the once-great glaciers are the ice sheets in the polar regions of Antarctica and most of Greenland. However, there was a period of unusually cold temperatures between 1550 and 1850. The river Thames in England froze over and glaciers advanced down into France. Yet this "Little Ice Age" was not considered a major ice age because most of the high

Slow Motion

Glaciers form in cold areas where temperatures are usually below 32°F (0°C), the freezing point of water. Over a period of fifty years or more, snowfalls can gradually build up layers of ice more than 13,000 feet (3,962 meters) thick. Huge masses of ice are heavy. Gravity causes glaciers to move downhill, carving out valleys as they go. Their flow is usually rather slow; the edge of a glacier moves about 2 feet (0.61 m) a day and up to 2 feet (0.61 m) a month. When glaciers reach the sea, pieces may break off and become floating icebergs.

mountains in the Northern Hemisphere were not covered with ice.

In 1920 Yugoslavian mathematician Milutin Milankovitch provided a theory that explained why ice ages come and go. He suggested that Earth's climate is determined by how much energy it receives from the sun. The tilt of Earth's axis produces seasons through the year. Areas near the equator receive the most direct sunlight. Areas near the North Pole and South Pole get the least. Areas in between get different amounts of sun, depending on how far north or south of the equator they are. And changes in Earth's tilt determine the strength of the seasons.

Collecting Evidence

How do we know what the climate was like millions of years ago? Scientists have pieced together a record of Earth's climate for the past 800 million years of its 4.6-billion-year history. Rock formations, fossils, and other bits of evidence reveal that Earth's climate has gone through major changes. For instance, a tree grows a new ring for each year it lives. Not only can a study of its rings show how old the tree is, the thickness of the rings may indicate the climate at that time. Thin rings, for example, may be a sign of poor growth due to droughts or severe spring frosts.

This ice core was drilled from Antarctica in 1993. The core was shipped to a laboratory where scientists studied the bubbles trapped in each layer of ice to learn more about past climates.

Ice samples (called ice cores) taken by drilling into glaciers in Greenland or Antarctica also give clues to past climates. Inside these chunks of ice are air bubbles (pockets of air) that have been trapped there for hundreds or even thousands of years. The gases in these air bubbles provide evidence of what the climate used to be and of the concentration of gases in the air at the time the bubbles were trapped. Scientists have also collected animal fossils found deep in the ocean floor. These specimens provide information about the temperatures of the oceans about 100 million years ago.

Milankovitch explained that Earth goes through changes according to fairly regular cycles. Every 100,000 years or so, Earth's orbit changes from an ellipse (oval) to a circular path. The minimum distance of the planet from the sun also increases. Meanwhile, every 41,000 years, the tilt of Earth's axis increases by a few degrees. A greater tilt brings more severe seasons: colder winters and warmer summers. Less tilt means less severe seasons: warmer winters and cooler summers. When summers are cool, less of the snow and ice left over from the winter melts, and ice sheets build up. Earth also wobbles on its axis like a spinning top over a period of about 22,000 years. This produces further changes in Earth's climate. (Currently we are in the part of this cycle that produces milder seasons in the Northern Hemisphere.)

Milankovitch calculated that whenever all three cycles (the change in orbit, tilt, and wobble) produce a drop in the amount of sunlight reaching the Northern Hemisphere, major ice sheets form. And so an ice age begins. We are currently in a warming period, but we can expect another ice age in the future. According to various estimates, the glaciers will return in about 60,000 to 100,000 years.

Volcanoes and Weather

Sometimes natural disasters such as erupting volcanoes can produce unexpected weather conditions in parts of the world. This happened in June 1991.

Above: *Mount Pinatubo erupts in 1991, spewing steam and ash into the air. The volcano in the Philippines exploded after being inactive for more than six hundred years.*

Right: *Many of the islands that make up the Philippines were covered in ash after Mount Pinatubo erupted. These houses and trees are gray with the ash.*

Mount Pinatubo, a volcano in the Philippines, exploded after being inactive for more than six hundred years. Loads of ash and debris thrown up into Earth's atmosphere changed weather patterns all over the world in 1992. The particulates (solid particles of soot, ash, and other substances) in the atmosphere blocked the sun's rays, making the weather cooler than usual. The extra particles in the air also caused large amounts of water vapor to condense, producing heavy rain or snowfalls. At the time, many people wondered what would happen to global warming. But the eruption of Mount Pinatubo just put a temporary halt to the world's warming trend.

Climate Models

Earth's climate is a very complex system. It is affected not only by the atmosphere but also by the oceans, ice sheets, land, soils, rocks, and every living thing on the planet. All these things, to some degree, move heat around Earth's surface. So many variables are involved in determining climate that it is difficult to get the whole picture. These days, scientists use computer models to learn more about the climate system, how it changes, and what the changes mean for the future.

Much of what we know about climate is based on plugging data into theoretical computer models. This information comes from various resources all over the world. These tools include ground and sea surface thermometers, tidal gauges, precipitation gauges, weather balloons, and satellites. Scientists study the information over a period of years and look for patterns that allow them to predict future climatic changes.

The most sophisticated computer model is called the general circulation model, or GCM. The GCM includes a three-dimensional computer map of the atmosphere, oceans, and landmasses. It is designed to model Earth's climate and to test its behavior when exposed to various conditions. For example, how would a major volcanic eruption affect the climate worldwide? What about a change in the radiation from the sun? Scientists can also vary the concentrations of gases in the computer model's atmosphere and study the effects on climate. This work has helped researchers understand how an excess of carbon dioxide can affect the conditions on our planet.

Computer models are far from perfect. They are only as good as the information that is entered. Before 1989, for example, most computer models didn't even include the effects of clouds, which are an important part of the

Did You Know?
Many of the measurements used in computer models are taken in cities. But city buildings and vehicles create trapped heat, which produces a "heat island" effect. This "heat island" effect can give a false impression of warming.

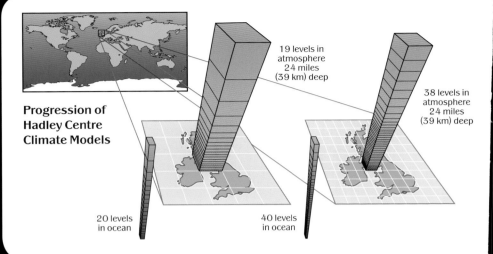

Progression of Hadley Centre Climate Models

19 levels in atmosphere 24 miles (39 km) deep

38 levels in atmosphere 24 miles (39 km) deep

20 levels in ocean

40 levels in ocean

This comparison of climate models from the Hadley Centre for Climate Prediction and Research in the United Kingdom shows one reason why climate models have improved over time. The model on the left dates back to 1999. The model on the right, from 2005, shows much more detail. The boxes in newer climate models represent smaller land areas and smaller volumes of air and water. This greater detail gives more accurate predictions of climate change.

climate system. Clouds can have two different effects on climate. Some clouds reflect the sun's radiation back into space, providing a cooling effect. Other clouds absorb the sun's energy, trapping heat close to Earth's surface. Ice cover also affects Earth's climate. The sun's rays bounce off its white surface and head back out into space, cooling Earth's surface. This cooling effect will decrease if the Arctic ice continues to melt. And in fact, the Arctic Ocean is the place on Earth that has been warming fastest.

The computer models are continually being improved and redesigned to include important factors that can affect climate. Such factors are various kinds of pollution, the different ways air is circulated across the globe, and changes in the sun's radiation, concentration of gases, and other variables.

Climatologists have begun using computer models to produce decade-long forecasts of climate changes. These forecasts are similar to the weeklong weather predictions on TV and Internet weather sites. In 2008 an important change was made in the model to make these ten-year forecasts more accurate. The new model included data on ocean temperatures to reflect the changing patterns of ocean currents. The researchers predicted a cooling trend for Europe and North America in the coming decade. Natural variations in Pacific Ocean temperatures had also shifted into a cooling phase. A decade of cooler temperatures will probably increase the number of people saying, "What happened to global warming?" But the scientists emphasize that these natural variations do not change the long-term trend of rising worldwide temperatures. After the cooling phase is over, we will be getting even hotter.

chapter five

Is Global Warming for Real?

It was not until 1860 that scientists started to keep track of temperatures around the world. Records show that the world's average temperature has increased by about 1°F (0.6°C) in the last century. Many scientists are convinced that this is a sign that global warming has begun. In fact, seven of the ten warmest years on record occurred during the 1990s. And some of the most severe weather conditions occurred during that decade.

Not everyone is convinced that global warming really exists, however. Even those who do agree that global warming is occurring do not all believe that humans are causing the problem. Some scientists say that the amount of gases we add to the atmosphere is insignificant compared to the amount produced by natural processes. Erupting volcanoes, for example, spew tons of gases and particulates into the atmosphere. Decaying plants and animals' digestive systems release large amounts of methane. Some scientists argue that recent severe weather patterns are more likely due to natural climatic cycles. Remember, Earth has gone through various warming and cooling periods for millions of years, and right now we seem to be in a warming pattern.

Rising Temperatures

Many climatologists believe that over the last ten thousand years, the average global temperature has remained fairly constant. It has varied by no more than 3 or 4°F (1.7 or 2.2°C). So scientists realized there could be a problem when records showed an increase of 1°F (0.6°C) in just a century.

The most noticeable signs of global warming seem to be in the colder regions. When temperatures rise, snow and ice melt. Areas such as Alaska, Canada, and northern Russia have experienced more warming than the entire planet. From 1970 to 2000, for example, the average temperature in Alaska increased by 5°F (2.8°C). Alaskan cruise ships used to stop close to the front of the Columbia Glacier, so passengers could watch icebergs break off and drop into Prince William Sound.

Columbia Glacier in Alaska has been retreating at a faster rate since 2001.

Above: *Chunks of ice breaking off the Columbia Glacier in Alaska have made it dangerous for tourist boats to pass close by.* Below: *The Aletsch Glacier in Switzerland is also retreating.*

Global Warming

Passengers can no longer do this, however. Chunks of ice are now breaking off more frequently, making the area too dangerous for passing ships. Nearly 10 miles (16 km) of the glacier's front have disappeared since 1982.

The warming temperatures have melted glaciers in other areas as well. During the twentieth century, the front of Aletsch Glacier in Switzerland retreated more than a mile (1.6 km), and the glacier lost more than 300 feet (91 m) in thickness. In 1850 Montana's Glacier National Park had one hundred fifty glaciers. Now there are only thirty-five! Scientists believe that practically all of the park's glaciers will be gone within the next several decades.

Satellite observations have reported that the Antarctic ice sheets are losing as much as 36 cubic miles of ice (150 cubic km) each year, and the ice is melting faster each

Rivers of meltwater cover the surface of the remaining Ward Hunt Ice Shelf in the Arctic. If temperatures in the Arctic keep rising, further breakup of the ice shelf is very likely.

year. The melting ice is already raising the level of the world's oceans by about 0.16 inch (0.4 millimeters) a year. That doesn't sound like much, but Antarctica contains about 90 percent of the world's ice. Scientists estimate that if just the West Antarctic Ice Sheet (a small part of the total) melted, it would raise worldwide sea levels by 20 feet (6 m).

These tilted and sinking power lines show that permafrost is melting along the Alaska Highway near the Canadian border.

Permafrost, soil in the Arctic regions that stays frozen all year round, is also showing signs of melting. During the summer, the soil above the permafrost thaws out, allowing plants to grow. An increase in average temperatures has caused the permafrost to thaw out, too, making areas of the ground soft and unstable. In parts of Alaska, melting patches of permafrost are causing forests to drown as they sink into the ground and are flooded with swamp water. Roadways have become cracked. Bridges and buildings are unstable and breaking apart as they sink into the ground. People have had to abandon their homes. At the same time, the melting permafrost is releasing carbon dioxide, methane, and other greenhouse gases that have been trapped in the frozen ice for thousands of years.

Rising Sea Levels

As Earth's atmosphere warms, so do the ocean waters. When ocean waters are warmed they expand, taking up more space and causing sea levels to rise. At the same time, melting glaciers and ice sheets also add more water to the seas. These two factors— expansion of ocean waters and melting ice sheets— both contribute to raising the sea level. In fact, we have already seen a rise in sea levels over the past century. Tidal gauges (instruments that measure sea levels)

Did You Know?
Computer models indicate that if the average global temperature rose by only 7°F (about 4°C), the sea level would be 16 feet (5 m) higher. That would drown entire cities. On the other hand, a 7°F (about 4°C) *drop* in the average global temperature would put our planet into another ice age.

recorded an average global rise of 6 to 8 inches (15 to 20 centimeters) during the twentieth century.

Coastal areas have already been greatly affected by the rising seas. For instance, parts of the coastline of the Strait of Georgia, near Vancouver, Canada, have been eroded by waves. Cliffs at Point Grey, also near Vancouver, have also been worn away by crashing waves. Coastal marshes, which are important habitats for waterfowl, salmon, and other wildlife, are being flooded by rising sea levels.

The cliffs at Point Grey, near Vancouver, Canada, have been eroded by waves crashing against them. Rising sea levels mean more coastal areas will be affected by erosion and flooding.

Living Evidence

Since 1959 German scientists have been recording the date of the first appearance of flowers in the spring and the turning of the leaves in the fall each year. In 1993 they determined that spring was arriving an average of six days earlier than it did in 1959. The beginning of fall was an average of five days later, as well. This means the growing season had increased by eleven days.

In 2001 satellite measurements confirmed this trend. Over the previous twenty years, places above 40 degrees latitude in the Northern Hemisphere (including New York, Madrid, Spain, and Beijing, China) had experienced healthier plant growth and a longer growing season. In the United States, the growing season had increased by nearly two weeks during that time.

The rising temperatures have produced changes in the behavior of a number of animal species, as well. In Great Britain, some amphibians are spawning earlier in the spring, and birds are laying their eggs earlier. Across Europe and North America, migrating birds have been spreading northward to take advantage of warmer living conditions.

Meanwhile, the changing climate has been taking a toll on some species that live in cold regions. Between 1970 and 2004, the population of emperor penguins on the Antarctic Peninsula decreased by 50 percent. Polar bears, which live on the Arctic ice, are also in danger. From 1987 to 2007, their population dropped from about 33,000 to 25,000. Arctic seals are in danger, too. They spend their first month of life burrowed in the ice while they grow the fat layers that help keep their bodies warm. But the melting of the Arctic ice sends baby seals out into the cold water before they have enough insulation to protect them. During the last century, the numbers of Arctic seals dropped from 180,000 to about 8,500.

Polar Bears' Plight

Polar bears spend much of the year out on floating sheets of sea ice. That is where they hunt seals and other prey. When the weather warms up, they move over to the ice-covered land nearby. (A large polar bear can swim up to 100 miles, or 160 km, kept warm by the layer of blubber under its skin.) Hunting is not very good on land, so the bears spend most of the warm season lying around and living on their stored fat. But the Arctic sea ice has been melting, and the distance to the coast is getting too far for the bears to swim. Many polar bears drown or freeze while trying to cross over. In May 2008, the U.S. Fish and Wildlife Service officially listed the polar bear as "threatened" under the Endangered Species Act.

Above: *Harbor seals like these are becoming rarer in the Arctic. Partly due to melting of Arctic ice, baby seals go out into the cold water before they are ready.*

Left: *Polar bears also face problems as temperatures warm and ice melts in the Arctic. Polar bears sometimes drown while trying to swim from floating sheets of ice to land.*

chapter six

The Effects of Global Warming

Is global warming as bad as they say? Some people would say no. Having a few extra days at the beach doesn't sound so bad. Heating bills would be lower, and we would have fewer snow-plowing expenses in the winter. (Air-conditioning expenses would go up in the summer, though.) People in colder regions might look forward to warming temperatures. Farmers would benefit from the longer growing seasons in a warmer climate.

Global warming is actually a bit more complicated, however. The effects on the climate would not be the same all over the world. That's because of the way wind and ocean currents move heat energy around the globe. If climatologists' projections are correct, some areas will experience heavy rainfalls, violent storms, and flooding, while others may not receive any rain at all. Global warming may actually cause some areas to get colder and produce heavy snowfalls. Whether the changes are considered good or bad, almost every place on Earth would experience a climate that is different from what it used to be.

Turning Up the Heat

In 2001 the Intergovernmental Panel on Climate Change (IPCC) published a report projecting that surface temperatures will likely increase by 2.5 to 10.4°F (1.4 to 5.8°C) by 2100. (The report did not, however, indicate which areas will be most affected by the warming.) As the world becomes warmer, we could expect hotter summers and warmer winters. Heat waves during the summer would be more frequent and last longer.

Extreme heat and humidity can be uncomfortable and downright miserable. For some people though, they can also cause serious health problems, such as a heart attack or breathing difficulties. Extreme heat can even cause death. In 1995 heat stroke killed more than 500 people in Chicago, Illinois, during a heat wave that lasted for days. In 2003 a record heat wave in Europe led to an estimated 35,000 deaths.

The heat wave in Europe in 2003 contributed to the deaths of thousands of elderly people in France.

When the mercury rises, so does the demand for air conditioning. The hotter it gets, the more people use their air conditioners. Air conditioners are run by electricity, but our power plants can make only a certain amount of electricity. When the demand becomes too great, the power supply drains very quickly until it becomes too low to support the widespread needs. As a result, an entire city could experience a "blackout"—no power at all. That's why it's not unusual for towns to request that people limit their energy usage during especially hot days. In recent years, blackouts have become more and

People at this California restaurant eat their dinner in the dark. The state sometimes schedules blackouts in the summer because of the high demand for electricity in the heat.

more frequent because of the warming temperatures.

At the same time, the increased air-conditioning also contributes to global warming. As we generate power to run the air conditioners, greenhouse gases are being produced and released into the atmosphere.

When the heat rages on, if rainfall is sparse, other problems can develop. The land becomes drier and drier, which makes it easier for the plant life to catch fire. Forest fires can spread quickly when the land is very dry. The fires, too, send greenhouse gases into the atmosphere.

Lakes and reservoirs also start to dry up, and water supplies become limited. In some parts of the United States, especially in the West and Southwest, droughts are common. Laws have been passed that limit how often people can water their lawns and that forbid restaurants to serve water unless the customer asks for it.

This lake in California has dried up.

Droughts are a serious problem for farmers who depend on the rain for their crops. They need rain to grow wheat, corn, and other important crops that we eat every day. When farmers are unable to produce enough crops, prices will go up.

While global warming would cause some regions in the world to experience droughts, others would receive more rain. In some areas, such as central Europe, farmers welcome this change. They would be able to grow more wheat, which is an important food source for millions of people. In some parts of Australia, warmer temperatures and increased rainfall have already led to record-high crops. Desert areas in the southwestern United States, northern Africa, and the Middle East might become good farmlands. In Canada, however, more rain would be disastrous. Too much rain would drown much of the wheat crop.

Overall, climate models project that global warming would lead to a small drop in crop production in the United States but an increase in much of the rest of the world.

Did You Know?
Higher levels of carbon dioxide in the atmosphere are not all bad. Carbon dioxide actually helps plants grow, which increases crop production.

Disease on the Rise

Disease-carrying insects and rodents thrive in tropical climates. As temperatures rise in colder regions, these disease carriers may spread to areas outside of their natural range. For example, malaria has been appearing in places where it had never existed before. Malaria, a serious illness that is common in tropical regions of Africa, Asia, and South and Central America, is caused by a tiny parasite spread by mosquitoes. The mosquitoes that carry malaria have expanded their range to parts of the world that used to be too cool for them. In the 1990s, cases of malaria were reported in Michigan, Texas, Georgia, California, New Jersey, and New York. However, these were just isolated cases, and the risk of malaria in the United States is still very low. Scientists are concerned that global warming may help the spread of other dangerous mosquito-borne diseases as well, including dengue fever, yellow fever, and encephalitis.

Warmer temperatures will also lengthen "tick season"—the time of the year when ticks are most active. Ticks, which thrive in warm, moist environments, can spread disease when they feed on an animal's blood. Different kinds of ticks spread different kinds of illnesses. The most common tick-borne disease is called Lyme disease. It is caused by a bacterium that

Ticks spread disease by feeding on animals' blood. When they bite humans, they can transfer diseases and germs they have picked up from these animals.

is spread to animals and people by deer ticks, which carry the Lyme disease bacterium. Deer ticks are very tiny, about the size of a poppy seed. They usually feed on deer and field mice. Some other tick-borne diseases are Rocky Mountain spotted fever, Colorado tick fever, tularemia, and relapsing fever.

Stormy Weather

Climatologists believe that the warmer ocean temperatures are intensifying a weather phenomenon called El Niño. El Niño is short for *El Niño de Navidad*, Spanish for "Christ child." It got its name because it occurs around Christmastime on the Pacific coast of South America. El Niño creates a change in the direction of winds and ocean currents, which makes for unusually warm waters in the southeastern tropical Pacific Ocean. Every three to seven years, El Niño causes some serious changes in the usual weather patterns all over the world. This has been occurring more frequently and more severely in recent years.

The effects of El Niño are often disastrous. Its arrival in the 1997–1998 winter season brought one of the most powerful storms on record to California. The state was flooded with heavy rains, strong winds, and 30-foot (9 m) waves along the coast. Railroads and highways were destroyed, hundreds of homes were demolished, and lives were lost. At the same time, other strange weather events affected different

Waves pound oceanfront homes during an El Niño-powered storm in southern California in December 1997.

parts of the United States. In Florida, a huge storm set off destructive tornadoes that tore up neighborhoods and killed more than forty people. In Ohio, heavy snowfalls covered parts of the state. However, in large areas of the eastern and north-central United States, people enjoyed the warmest winter in years, bringing early flower blossoms.

In the past, very powerful El Niño effects were observed, on average, every forty-two years. Recently, however, the pattern seems to be speeding up. Strong El Niño effects, with violent storms and severe damage, occurred in 1982–1983 and again in 1997–1998, only fifteen years later.

Climate models predict that global warming will bring storms that are more severe, more often, even when El Niño effects are not occurring. Severe storms would bring periodic floods and severe wind damage to many regions. Areas such as the southeastern United States, which already experience frequent storms during the hurricane season of the late summer and early fall, would be especially hard hit. In August 2005, for example, New Orleans, Louisiana, was hit by one of the worst hurricanes in U.S. history. Hurricane Katrina brought powerful winds, with gusts up to 125 miles per hour (201 km/hr). The whipping winds lifted the water of the lakes and rivers and pushed it to the shore. These rising waters, called storm surges, flooded coastal areas. In just a matter of hours, the flood waters destroyed homes, roads, bridges,

This satellite image of Hurricane Katrina shows the storm bearing down on Louisiana and Mississippi in August 2005.

Debris caused by damage from Hurricane Ike piled up on streets in Galveston, Texas, in 2008.

hospitals, and schools in Louisiana, Mississippi, and Alabama. The storm surges reached more than 27 feet (8 m) in some areas. There were 1,836 confirmed deaths. In New Orleans, storm surges flooded about 80 percent of the city. Climatologists expect that global warming will make hurricanes and other major storms not only more frequent but also more violent, possibly as dangerous as Hurricane Katrina. In September 2008, for example, two major hurricanes struck the Gulf Coast within two weeks. Hurricane Gustav hit New Orleans, and then Hurricane Ike slammed into Galveston, Texas. Ike caused

Did You Know?
New Orleans has a higher than average risk of flooding because the city lies in a bowl-shaped area, from 6 to 20 feet (2 to 6 m) *below* sea level.

widespread flooding and destruction in Galveston and Houston, Texas, and knocked out electric power throughout most of Texas.

Low-Lying Lands Are Threatened

Climate models indicate that we can expect sea levels to rise even further—from 8 inches (0.2 m) to as much as 7 feet (2 m)—by the year 2050. This would have a serious impact on coastal cities and low-lying countries, such as Bangladesh, the Netherlands, and the Maldive Islands (located in the Indian Ocean). Most of the 1,190 islands that make up the Maldives are less than 6 feet (1.8 m) above sea level. So it

These palm trees on the coast of the Maldive Islands are so close to the shore that they are falling into the Indian Ocean.

wouldn't take much for rising waters to overwhelm these islands and force the thousands of inhabitants to abandon their homes. Some of these countries are too poor to build walls to protect them from the rising seas.

Closer to home, some coastal areas of the United States are currently just about at sea level. A significant rise in the ocean levels could put cities like New York City and the entire state of Florida underwater. Rising waters could also flood coastal marshes and swamps, wiping out whole ecosystems.

Species Are in Danger

Throughout history, many living creatures have been able to adapt to changes in the environment. Many, however, have not. In fact, scientists believe that 99.9 percent of all the species that have ever lived on Earth are now extinct! Changes in the past have been slow and gradual, occurring over hundreds or thousands of years. But changes brought on by global warming have been far more rapid. And they are speeding up. Many species may not be able to adapt and survive. About 30,000 species are becoming extinct each year. Various human activities are causing this huge die-off. But scientists estimate that global warming alone could wipe out more than one-third of Earth's living species by the end of the twenty-first century.

The ringed seals of Lake Saimaa, in Finland, are down to about 250 individuals. They are the most endangered seal in the world. It has been a difficult struggle to keep these seals from becoming extinct. This endangered species is faced with a major threat from global warming. Normally, Saimaa ringed seals give birth to their cubs in a den made of snow, which

Salmon spawn (lay eggs) in the Adams River in British Columbia, Canada. Reduced water levels in rivers due to climate change can make spawning difficult for salmon.

protects them from the cold weather and predators. But there is not enough snow for their dens, and many cubs cannot survive into adulthood. If the warming continues, the Saimaa seal population may become extinct.

Many cold-water animals are also in danger as temperatures of streams, rivers, and oceans rise.

Salmon, for example, are cold-blooded, and temperature plays an important role in their survival. Cooler temperatures allow salmon to use their energy more efficiently. When the water temperature gets warmer, the fish need more food to live. After a while, they can't keep up with their bodies' needs, and they die.

Salmon are born in a freshwater stream, and most of them swim downstream to live in the saltwater of the ocean. When they are ready to reproduce, they swim back upstream, as far as 2,000 miles (3,220 km) away from the ocean. The warming temperatures, however, may interrupt the salmon's annual spawning (laying of their eggs). In the Pacific Northwest, rivers and streams are fed by melting snow in the summers. Warmer winters bring more rain and less snow. This climate change can result in flooding in the winter, which can tear up the nests where the females lay their eggs. Reduced water levels in the summer can also make spawning difficult.

As the oceans continue to get warmer, salmon will have to swim farther north to the Bering Sea, to find the cooler waters they need. However, they may not be able to survive the long migration back when it is time to spawn.

Warming ocean temperatures are harming populations of krill, a shrimplike sea creature. Krill is an important food source for penguins, whales, and many kinds of fish and seabirds. Without krill many of these animals may not survive, while others are likely to move to cooler waters.

Coral reefs are also threatened by warming temperatures. Corals are tiny soft-bodied sea animals covered with stony skeletons made of calcium carbonate (limestone). Corals take calcium out of the seawater to form their limestone skeletons. These living corals are known as polyps. Most coral polyps live together in colonies. They attach themselves to each other and form coral reefs, which consist of both living and dead polyps. When the polyps die, their skeletons remain, solidifying the reef. Coral reefs are of different sizes, shapes, and colors, depending on the species.

The contrast between bleached coral (left) *and healthy coral* (right) *is obvious in this photo of a coral reef near a tropical island in the Pacific Ocean.*

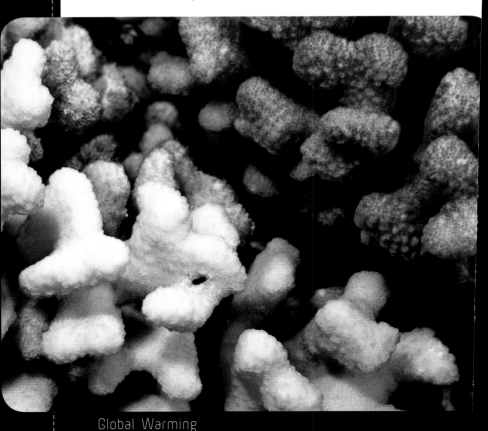

Single-celled algae (plantlike microorganisms), growing inside the corals, help the corals by supplying them with important nutrients they need to survive. Corals are very sensitive to rising ocean temperatures. As water temperatures warm, the corals become stressed and lose many of the algae that provide them with food and color. Researchers have found that warmer waters help bacteria that infect the algae to spread. Under stress, the corals get rid of dead or infected algae. Without the algae, the corals appear white, or "bleached." Many coral reefs did not survive the arrival of El Niño in 1997–1998. Many more are dying as water temperatures continue to rise. Some corals, however, can recover when conditions become less stressed. New algae move in. The corals regain their color and become healthy again.

chapter seven

Can Global Warming Be Stopped?

According to a poll taken in 2008, less than half of

the people in the United States believe that human

activities are the main cause of global warming. Most

people do agree, however, that the warming trend is

real and that carbon dioxide and other greenhouse

gases are contributing to the problem.

So what should we do about it? Do we need to do anything now, or should we just wait and see how severe the problem becomes? Most Americans seem to feel that doing something about global warming is not very urgent. In one 2008 opinion poll, those questioned ranked global warming fifteenth out of twenty-one problems facing Americans. Issues such as crime and terrorism were rated much higher. In another poll reported in January 2008, only 35 percent thought global warming should be a top priority for the president and Congress that year.

The problem with the "wait and see" attitude is that most *scientists* believe that global warming is real and is due to human activities. They say that if we don't do anything, the greenhouse gases will build up and global warming will increase. Eventually we may reach a point at which the problem *can't* be fixed. In fact, some scientists think we may have already reached that point.

Projections suggest that the most devastating effects of global warming are not likely to occur in the near future. So why should we worry about it? Because what we decide now will affect future generations. They will have to live in the world we create.

Taking action against global warming will cost money. For example, fossil fuels are the cheapest energy sources at present. Switching to cleaner-burning fuels and more energy-efficient machines would be expensive. Who should pay for the costs? Should private individuals and companies bear the burden, or should the government help out? How should the cost be shared among the various countries of the world?

Smoke billows into the air at this coal-burning power station in Yunnan, China. Coal-burning power stations release vast amounts of CO_2 into the atmosphere.

A Global Effort

The actions of one nation alone cannot stop global warming. No matter where they are produced, greenhouse gases pass into the atmosphere, and their effects can be felt around the globe. Therefore, we need the cooperation of nations all over the world—especially the developed countries. Their industries and technology produce substantial amounts of greenhouse gas emissions.

In 1992 representatives from about 170 nations, including the United States, met in Rio de Janeiro, Brazil, at the Earth Summit. They signed the United Nations Framework Convention on Climate Change (UNFCCC). This agreement called for voluntary action to cut the production of greenhouse gases to 1990 levels by the year 2000. The agreement didn't work, though. Carbon dioxide emissions continued to increase, especially among the industrialized nations. (By 1995 U.S. emissions were more than 10 percent higher than they had been in 1990.)

In 1997 a new meeting was held in Kyoto, Japan. Representatives from more than 160 nations agreed on a new policy they called the Kyoto Protocol. This agreement required thirty-eight industrialized nations to cut their production of carbon dioxide

The Earth Summit in Brazil in 1992 brought world leaders together to talk about climate change.

emissions and five other greenhouse gases to 5.2 percent below 1990 levels by the years 2008 to 2012. Developing countries, however, would not have any restrictions on their carbon dioxide emissions.

In March 2001, the United States withdrew from the Kyoto agreement. President George W. Bush called the treaty "fatally flawed." He argued that the targets were unrealistic and that such restrictions would be too costly for the U.S. economy. Other critics of the plan pointed out that major developing countries, such as China, India, Indonesia, Mexico, and Brazil, should have their carbon dioxide emissions limited, too. In fact, industrialization and carbon dioxide emissions in the developing countries have expanded even more rapidly than these critics feared.

It was clear that the Kyoto agreement wasn't working, but many nations were not ready to give up. They believed that the important thing was to get some kind of agreement, even if it meant aiming for smaller cuts in emissions.

Big Polluters

At the end of the twentieth century, the production of greenhouse gases per person in the United States was twice the amount produced per person in Japan, three times the amount in France, and ten times the amount in Brazil. The United States, with just 5 percent of the world's population, accounted for 25 percent of the greenhouse gases released in the atmosphere, making it the world's biggest polluter.

However, the situation has changed rapidly. China, India, and other developing nations have made a big effort to catch up industrially. They have been building new factories, powered by the cheapest and most readily available fuels—mainly coal. By 2006 China had become the new world leader in greenhouse gas emissions. That year, China sent 6.2 billion tons (5.6 billion metric tons) of carbon dioxide into the atmosphere, compared to 5.8 billion tons (5.3 billion metric tons) of carbon dioxide emissions produced in the United States.

Above: *A power plant in Mongolia emits large amounts of CO_2.* **Left:** *Pollution hangs in the air over Mumbai, India. Many countries around the world are working on the problem of global warming. Efforts include trying to reduce emissions from power plants.*

In July 2001, representatives of 180 nations met in Bonn, Germany, and worked out a new agreement. The most developed nations would aim at reducing carbon dioxide emissions to 1.8 percent below the 1990 levels. A fund was established to help developing countries to clean up their emissions, so that they could someday join the treaty. Nations such as Japan, Canada, and Russia could get special credits against their carbon emission limits for managing their forests responsibly and planting new forests. Planting new forests would provide more carbon sinks that would soak up extra carbon dioxide.

Energy Alternatives

It's not going to be easy to change our energy practices. Most of the world relies on fossil fuels to generate energy. But fossil fuels are responsible for most of the human-produced carbon dioxide released into the atmosphere. And so we need to switch from fossil fuels to cleaner, more efficient energy sources.

Coal, the "dirtiest" fossil fuel, accounts for half of the carbon dioxide sent into the atmosphere by human activities. Oil also produces a lot of carbon dioxide, although not as much as coal. Natural gas is the cleanest fossil fuel, releasing half as much carbon dioxide as coal for each unit of energy produced. For this reason, some people suggest switching from coal and oil to natural gas. There are some problems associated with natural gas, however. For example, methane is a component of natural gas. Leaks from pipelines and storage facilities may release enough methane to counteract the benefits of using this energy source. (Remember, methane traps more heat than carbon dioxide.)

Researchers are working very hard to find alternative sources of energy. Nuclear energy is one possibility. It does not release any carbon dioxide or other greenhouse gases into the atmosphere. France offers a good example of nuclear power at work. Nuclear power plants provide

Researchers are looking for energy alternatives to coal mining and carbon dioxide-spewing power plants, both shown above.

about three-quarters of that country's electricity. Many people in the United States, however, have serious concerns about using nuclear energy. Critics say that it is very dangerous, and safely disposing of the radioactive wastes can be a costly and difficult problem. Terrorists might steal radioactive materials for use as weapons or sabotage nuclear power plants to cause devastating explosions. Building nuclear power plants is also very expensive. The United States has more than one hundred working nuclear power plants, but more than one hundred plant constructions have been canceled since 1974.

Nuclear power plants have gained a bad reputation since the accident at Three Mile Island, Pennsylvania, in 1979 and the disaster at Chernobyl in the Soviet Union (present-day Ukraine) in 1986. The power plant at Three Mile Island was permanently shut down after equipment

The 1986 disaster at the Chernobyl nuclear power plant in Ukraine caused an increase in cancer cases and destroyed communities in and around Chernobyl.

failure and human errors led to a partial meltdown of the reactor core. No one was injured or killed by this accident. A meltdown at Chernobyl, however, had disastrous effects. Tons of dangerous radioactive materials spewed out on the local area and reached surrounding countries as well. In addition to those injured and killed in the accident, radiation caused hundreds of cancer cases over the following decade. An increase in the leukemia rate was also suspected. Whole communities in the area around Chernobyl were destroyed. About 130,000 people had to leave their homes because it was no longer safe to live there or grow crops on the contaminated soil.

Time's Running Out

Fossil fuels are nonrenewable, or limited, sources of energy. Meanwhile, the more complex modern society becomes, the more fuel we use to support our needs. As a result, we are draining our fossil fuel reserves at a tremendous rate. It took thousands of years for these fossil fuels to form, but we may use them up within just a few centuries. Nuclear energy is also a limited energy source, relying on uranium mined from underground ore deposits. So scientists are concentrating on renewable resources—energy that never runs out, such as solar, wind, water, and even heat energy buried deep inside Earth.

Supporters of nuclear power plants say that the dangers are exaggerated. There are 434 active nuclear power plants in the world. With the exception of Three Mile Island and Chernobyl, these plants have had good safety records. In 2000 two people died at a nuclear power plant in Japan. And yet, far more people die from mining coal than from working in nuclear power plants. In 2006 forty-seven coal miners died in the United States. In China, the world's largest coal producer, the number of deaths in coal mines that same year was

China is the world's largest coal producer. It is building more nuclear power plants such as this one to meet the country's growing energy needs.

much higher—4,746.
However, fears about
nuclear energy may
prevent wider use of this
alternative energy source.

Energy from the Sun

This house has solar panels on the roof that absorb energy from the sun.

Solar energy is a renewable resource—we get a new supply from the sun each day. Scientists have learned how to capture the sun's energy and use it for our own needs. For instance, solar panels can be seen on the roofs of some buildings. The panels absorb energy from sunlight, which can be used to heat homes, boil water, and to make electricity.

Solar energy can be converted into electricity through a device called a photovoltaic cell, or solar cell. The materials in a solar cell produce an electric current when light shines on them. Large numbers of solar cells can be connected to form a solar battery. Low-power solar batteries are used to power calculators, watches, and cameras. More powerful solar batteries provide electricity for space satellites and have been used in experimental airplanes and automobiles.

Photovoltaic cells can help to reduce the carbon dioxide in the atmosphere. Electricity generated by photovoltaic cells can be used to break water molecules into two hydrogen atoms and one oxygen atom. The freed hydrogen gas could then replace the polluting carbon-based fuels that are presently used to fuel automobiles, homes, and factories. Hydrogen gas is much cleaner than fossil fuels. When hydrogen gas is burned, it recombines with oxygen in the atmosphere, forming water.

Photovoltaic cells are just starting to become competitive with oil. Eventually, as this technology improves, photovoltaic hydrogen systems could replace fossil fuels. This would have great benefits. The use of photovoltaic hydrogen fuel is harmless to the environment and would also make many nations less dependent on foreign energy sources.

Power generated by photovoltaic cells is more expensive than power produced by burning fossil fuels. As the market for solar energy grows, however, and more solar devices are made, the cost for each solar cell will drop. But why would people switch to solar energy if it is more expensive than oil, gas, or electric power sources? Many local regions and even whole nations are offering incentives for people to install solar devices. These include government loans, tax deductions, and rebates.

Germany has become the leading user of solar power in the world, as a result of its national Electricity Feed Law. When rooftop solar panels create more electricity than a building needs, the excess is sent to the electric power grid supplying the local area. Homeowners get a credit on their electric bill for the extra energy they supply. (In some cases, the credits are bigger than the bill!) Similar electricity feed-in laws and regulations are helping the growth of solar energy in countries such as Spain, Denmark, and Italy, and in some parts of the United States and Canada.

This office building in Heidelberg, Germany, has solar cells on the roof to use the sun's energy to provide power for the building.

Solar thermal (heating) systems are already much more widespread than solar panels with photovoltaic cells. These systems collect sunlight energy and use it directly to heat water. The hot water can be used for washing and bathing, or sent through radiators to warm buildings. In Germany, all new homes built from 2009 on must use renewable energy sources to provide at least 14 percent of the energy used for heating and hot water. From 2010 on, owners of older houses will have to add renewable-energy heating systems to provide at least 10 percent of their heating and hot water needs. The government is providing grants to help homeowners pay for the remodeling. Those who don't convert their heating systems will pay a fine. In the United

States, more than 1.2 million buildings have solar water-heating systems, and there are about 250,000 solar-heated swimming pools.

Other Alternative Energy Sources

Wind is another renewable energy source. Windmills, or wind turbines, tap into the wind's energy. Have

Wind turbines stand out against a blue sky. Using wind energy is one way people can cut down on air pollution.

Tennessee's Cherokee Dam supplies hydroelectric power using the power of falling water.

you ever blown on the sails of a pinwheel and watched them fly around in a circle? That is what a wind turbine looks like. Wind moves the sails of the wind turbine, which then produces electricity.

Water power is another old-fashioned energy source that holds promise for the future. Ocean waves crashing against rocks and waterfalls cascading downward hold enormous amounts of energy. One way to use this power is through waterwheels. The movement of water is used to drive turbines, which generate electricity. Hydroelectric power dams—*hydro* means "water"—use the force of falling water to run turbines. This is a cheap and efficient energy source, but building dams has huge effects on the surrounding environment.

This turbine is part of the tidal power plant on the Rance River in northwestern France.

A different kind of force causes the tides that flow through the seas and oceans. The tides rise and fall under the pull of the moon's gravity. The power of waves can be used to run turbines. In 1966 a plant that used tidal power was opened in France. This is the only major tidal power plant in the world. Others, which generate less electricity, can be found in Canada, Russia, and China. Tidal power plants are very expensive to build, which may be why there are not many of them.

Geothermal energy is another naturally occurring energy source, and the supply is practically limitless. Deep within Earth lies a thick layer of hot gases and molten rock called magma. The temperature of this magma is about 3,000°F (1,650°C). Magma may escape from inside Earth's interior when volcanoes erupt and ooze out lava, releasing magma gases. Sometimes hot water or steam may shoot out from tiny cracks in the Earth's surface and create hot springs. Animals, such as the Florida manatee, retreat to these hot springs during migration so they can stay warm. The ancient Romans used hot springs to warm their baths, and they are used in modern Iceland to heat buildings.

Hot springs do not occur everywhere. But geothermal energy can be tapped by drilling down to the hot rock, especially in places like Japan, the Philippines, California, and the west coast of South America, where the magma is closer to the surface. Water is sent down into the holes and is superheated, then turns into steam as it rises. The steam

Bathers relax in warm waters outside a geothermal plant in Iceland.

is used to turn turbines to generate electricity. One problem is that geothermal power plants may give off sulfur compounds. They not only smell like rotten eggs but also contribute to acid rain. This can destroy forests and damage buildings. Engineers are currently developing ways to filter out the sulfur gases. In most parts of the world, geothermal energy is still more expensive than fossil fuels. But it is a promising energy source for the future.

Scientists continue to research possible alternative energy sources. It may be a long time, though, before we can find acceptable replacements for fossil fuels that can be widely available to the whole world.

Improving Carbon Dioxide Sinks

Most of the plans for curbing global warming have focused on ways to reduce emissions of greenhouse gases. But there are natural processes that serve as sinks, removing carbon dioxide and other gases from the atmosphere. One of the most important is photosynthesis by plants.

Earth's forests are a major carbon dioxide sink. But even individual trees can help in lowering the amount of this greenhouse gas in the atmosphere. A study reported in 2007, for example, found that the trees in New York City remove 1,984 tons (1,800 metric tons) of CO_2 from the city's atmosphere. They also help reduce energy use by providing shade. However, U.S. cities have lost more than 20 percent of their trees since 1998. Environmental planners and forest researchers are studying local tree species to determine which trees remove and store carbon dioxide most effectively. One of the best in the New York area is the sycamore. Replanting trees in city streets is a good way to fight global warming and make the air quality healthier for the people who live there.

A team of scientists in Greifswald, Germany, has suggested that one solution to the global warming problem would be to plant forests of trees and then bury the wood in old coal pits

In New York City, the trees in Central Park contribute to keeping air pollution down.

and other surface mines. The trees would take carbon dioxide out of the air as they grew. After they were cut down, burying them would keep this gas from being returned to the atmosphere. A covering of soil would protect the wood from the weather. It would be a resource of building materials that could be dug up and used as needed.

Photosynthesis by plants and plantlike organisms in the oceans (phytoplankton) also serves as a huge carbon dioxide sink. Researchers have discovered that iron compounds can act like fertilizer for the phytoplankton of the oceans' surface waters, sparking an explosion of growth. In an experiment in the mid-1990s, scientists spread small amounts of iron sulfate over a 100-square-mile (259 sq. km) area of the Pacific Ocean near the equator. Within five days, the water had turned from electric blue to bright green, as the phytoplankton multiplied. Thousands of tons of extra plankton were produced. They removed about 2,500 tons (2,265 metric tons) of carbon dioxide from the atmosphere in two weeks.

The fast-growing phytoplankton die off after awhile. Some of them sink down to the deep ocean waters, removing CO_2 from the atmosphere for decades or even centuries. But fish feed on phytoplankton. When the fish die, their soft bodies are broken down by bacteria, releasing carbon dioxide back into the atmosphere. Many environmentalists have doubts about whether this "solution" to global warming is realistic.

In 2007 several companies announced plans to start large-scale ocean fertilization projects. Meanwhile, India planned a large-scale test of its own with the help of ocean scientists from Germany, Italy, and Chile. The research team would spread 22 tons (20 metric tons) of iron sulfate over a 386-square-mile (1,000 sq. km) area of the South Atlantic during the first three months of 2009.

Algae growing in freshwater ponds and lakes also help to soak up carbon dioxide in nature's carbon cycle. Researchers have already been studying algae as a source of biodiesel, a renewable energy source that can be used to replace fossil fuels.

This lake in Denmark has green algae on its surface. Algae like this can help absorb carbon dioxide from the air.

Getting Rid of CO$_2$

Some scientists have suggested removing carbon dioxide from the atmosphere and storing it under high pressure in underground caves. Others have ideas for turning it into a useful product. Skyonic, a Texas company, has developed a process that captures 90 percent of the carbon dioxide emitted by factory smokestacks and mixes it with lye to make baking soda. In addition to its uses in baking, absorbing odors in the refrigerator, and other household chores, baking soda is used in industry to grind or polish objects. Making it out of smokestack emissions is much cheaper than mining it. The process also removes metal and other pollutants from the emissions and produces valuable by-products including chlorine and hydrogen.

In 2008 XL Renewables, a company based in Phoenix, Arizona, opened a 40-acre (16 hectare) production site. Algae are grown there and converted to three useful products: not only biodiesel but also edible oils and high-protein animal feed. The company planned to develop a 400-acre (162 hectare) algae farm in 2009 that would produce and process more than 20,000 tons (18,145 metric tons) of algae per year.

What about methane? Researchers are also studying ways to reduce the amounts of this powerful greenhouse gas. Scientists from Leipzig, Germany, and the California Institute of Technology have discovered deep-sea bacteria that live on methane. This gas seeps out of the ocean floor, but most of it never reaches the atmosphere. About 80 percent of the deep-sea methane is immediately gobbled up by the bacteria. The researchers have identified all the genes that allow the bacteria to "burn" methane deep in the sea, where there is little or no oxygen. They have also worked out how the bacteria fit into the community of deep-sea microorganisms. In the future, these bacteria might be genetically changed to live in other methane-rich environments, such as swamps and cattle feedlots. Or the methane-burning genes could be transferred to other organisms as well.

Meanwhile, researchers in Australia and New Zealand are developing "burpless" grass that will cut down the amount of methane cows burp up when they chew their cud. Methane is produced as a byproduct when microorganisms in a cow's stomach break down plant matter. The researchers are changing the genes of the grass to make it more digestible. The cows that eat it won't have to chew and burp as much.

These are some of the things governments and scientists are working on to reduce the amounts of greenhouse gases in the atmosphere. But there are also important ways individual people—no matter their age or where they live—can help to control global warming.

chapter eight

A Green Future

For years, many scientists have been warning the public about global warming. For the most part, however, people have ignored these warnings. It wasn't until 2006 that global warming gained widespread, global attention with the documentary film *An Inconvenient Truth*. The film, featuring former U.S. vice president Al Gore, won an Oscar.

Gore discusses scientific evidence for global warming and the role that humans play in adding to the warming of the planet. If we do not reduce the billions of tons of carbon dioxide we produce every year, he argues, the effects could be disastrous. The film's message was loud and clear. We need to conserve energy *now* for our future generations.

Going Green

An Inconvenient Truth really made the general public think. Soon many people became enthusiastic about going green—that is, conserving energy and reducing pollution to help the environment. "Green" has become the new buzzword—a synonym for environmentally friendly. People can buy products made from recycled materials or renewable resources. For example, people can buy clothing made of cotton or wool instead of synthetic materials made from petroleum. They can recycle their paper or plastic grocery bags. Or better yet, they can take along a reusable cloth bag when they go to the supermarket.

Not just individuals are "going green" these days. Since 2000, for example, New York City has been switching its diesel-fueled buses to

Above: *Al Gore* (left) *and director Davis Guggenheim pose with the Academy Award for Best Documentary Feature for 2006. Their film* An Inconvenient Truth *had won the Oscar.* Below: *A woman hands a grocery store clerk her reusable cloth bags for her groceries.*

This hybrid bus transports people in the Minneapolis–Saint Paul, Minnesota, area.

a cleaner-burning fuel with 90 percent less sulfur. Effective filters have also helped to reduce polluting emissions from the diesel buses. By the end of 2007, more than five hundred new buses had hybrid engines, burning much less fossil fuel. Other cities across the United States are also replacing their bus fleets with diesel-electric hybrids. The new buses cost more than the old diesel buses, but they are quieter, more efficient, and much kinder to the environment. Many communities are also installing pollution-trapping filters on their diesel school buses.

Some large companies are taking steps to cut down pollution from industrial and agricultural machines. The Wal-Mart corporation, for example, has begun using forklifts that run on fuel cells in its big distribution centers. Older forklifts, used to move heavy loads, were powered by less efficient and more polluting diesel engines.

You Can Make a Difference

Governments are trying to work out a suitable energy plan on a global level. But there are many things that you can do on your own to lower emission levels and help the environment in the process. They include the following:

- Cut down on your use of electricity—turn off the lights, the computer, or the television when you are not using them. (Generating the electricity adds greenhouse gases to the atmosphere.)
- Use energy-saving fluorescent lightbulbs. They give off the same amount of light and use less energy than

Left: Leaving computers and other appliances on when they are not in use wastes electricity. Below: *Fluorescent lightbulbs are an energy-saving alternative.*

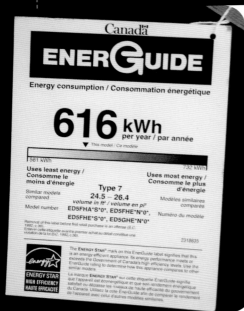

Many appliances come with the Energy Star label (bottom left in photo). *This means the product is designed to save energy.*

incandescent lightbulbs. And because they last longer, they are actually less expensive to use. (Incandescent lightbulbs will not be sold in the United States after 2014.)

- Buy energy-efficient machines and appliances. Look for the Energy Star label. It means that the product is designed to save energy. More efficient Energy Star products and building designs are already reducing carbon dioxide emissions by more than 15 million tons (14 metric tons) a year.

- Recycle newspapers, glass containters, aluminum cans, corrugated cardboard, and plastics instead of throwing them away. More energy is needed to produce new materials from scratch than

Did You Know?

In 2006 recycling programs in the United States collected 82 million tons (74 metric tons) of material. That's way up from 1990's total of 34 million tons (31 metric tons).

from recycled materials. An even better way to reduce greenhouse emissions, however, is by reducing the amount of waste you create in the first place.

- "eCycle" your family's old computers, cell phones, and other electronic devices. Manufacturers and stores are working with the U.S. Environmental Protection Agency (EPA) to collect old electronic devices. They donate them to schools and other public-service programs, or recycle their valuable materials (such as copper and gold), to save energy and prevent pollution. If all the cell phones thrown away in the United States in 2006 had been recycled, for example, the energy saved could have powered nearly 260,000 homes for a year!

Cell phones, along with other electronics, can be recycled instead of thrown in the garbage and taken to a landfill.

- Avoid gas-guzzling family cars. Instead, consider energy-efficient cars that don't use a lot of gasoline to drive long distances. Hybrid cars, which get great gas mileage on a limited amount of gasoline, are growing in popularity.
- Try walking, riding a bike, or taking the bus instead of having someone drive you to places that are not far, such as the corner store or your friend's house down the street.
- Eat meat less often, to decrease the numbers of methane-burping cattle.
- Make sure your home is energy-efficient. Walls and ceilings should be insulated. Use caulk or weather stripping around windows and doorways. Your power company can do an energy audit: Someone comes to your house and points out where energy might be escaping. You use more fuel when your house is not energy-efficient.
- Don't let the water faucet run too long while washing your hands in the bathroom at home.

Above: *The Toyota Prius cars are popular hybrid vehicles. They run on gasoline and battery power.* **Left:** *Riding a bicycle or walking instead of driving places that aren't very far is a great way to save energy. Taking the bus to places farther away helps too.*

Do the same at school, the mall, restaurant, or any other place. (Wasting water means wasting electricity.)

- Take shorter showers. You'll use less hot water. Water heaters make up almost 25 percent of your home's energy use.
- Turn off the tap when you brush your teeth.
- Turn off battery-operated toys or games when you are done with them. The batteries will last longer, so you won't have to replace them as often.

Planting trees is just one way people can do something to help the planet.

Whenever you save energy or use it more efficiently, you reduce the demand for gasoline, oil, coal, and natural gas. That means there will be less burning of fossil fuels, which in turn means less carbon dioxide emissions. All these solutions, such as the various energy-saving tips and even planting trees around your home, are not only good for you and your family but good for our planet, too.

Glossary

atmosphere: a mixture of gases (including nitrogen, oxygen, carbon dioxide, and water vapor) that surrounds Earth

biodiesel: a form of fuel similar to diesel but made from algae or plant matter instead of petroleum

carbon dioxide: a chemical compound containing two atoms of oxygen bonded to each atom of carbon. It is a gas present in the atmosphere, which is produced by burning of fuels and used in photosynthesis by plants.

carbon dioxide sink: a natural process that removes carbon dioxide from the atmosphere. Plant life and oceans are important carbon dioxide sinks.

CFCs (chlorofluorocarbons): powerful greenhouse gases produced by humans and formerly used as coolants

climate: the pattern of weather conditions typical of a particular area

climatologist: a scientist who studies climate

condensation: a change of state of matter from liquid to solid or gas to liquid

deforestation: the removal of forests or trees

El Niño: a cyclic change in the world's weather patterns due to a change in the direction of the winds and ocean currents

emit: release, give off gases or radiation. *Emissions* are the gases that are released into the atmosphere.

evaporation: a change of state from a liquid to a gas

fossil fuels: coal, oil, and natural gas, formed from the remains of ancient organisms buried by soil and rock and used as an energy source

general circulation model (GCM): climate model designed to simulate Earth's climate and to test its behavior when exposed to various conditions; includes a three-dimensional computer map of the atmosphere, oceans, and landmasses

geothermal energy: energy obtained from the hot matter inside Earth

glacier: a large mass of ice covering an extensive area of land or water and formed from the accumulation of snow over many years

global warming: a worldwide increase in Earth's average temperature

gravity: a force of attraction between two objects; the attractive force that holds objects to Earth's surface

greenhouse effect: a warming of Earth due to atmospheric gases such as carbon dioxide, which trap heat like the glass in a greenhouse

greenhouse gases: heat-trapping gases involved in the greenhouse effect

humidity: amount of water vapor in the air

ice ages: periods when Earth experiences extremely cold weather and when much of its surface is covered by snow and ice

infrared radiation: heat energy

interglacial period: a time of warmer temperatures between ice ages

magma: a thick layer of hot gases and molten rock deep inside Earth

methane: a greenhouse gas (CH_4) produced by natural processes and human activities

ozone: a highly reactive form of oxygen. In the atmosphere, it traps part of the energy from sunlight.

particulates: soot, ash, and other solid particles that are a component of air pollution

permafrost: frozen soil in the Arctic regions

photosynthesis: a process in which plants and certain bacteria use sunlight energy to convert carbon dioxide and water to complex carbon compounds. These products are used as food and building materials. Oxygen is produced as a by-product.

photovoltaic cell: a device that converts solar energy into electricity; also called a solar cell

phytoplankton: plantlike organisms that grow in surface waters of oceans

retreat: relating to glaciers, to melt and consequently cover a smaller land area

rotate: turn around on an axis

solar thermal system: a system with solar panels to collect sunlight energy and use it directly to heat hot water instead of converting it to electricity

tidal power: use of the energy of moving water produced by the gravitational pull of the moon to create electricity

ultraviolet radiation (UV rays): radiation just beyond the violet edge of visible light; a natural part of sunlight. UV rays contain more energy than visible light and can damage skin and eyes.

water cycle: the successive processes of evaporation, condensation, and precipitation that keep water circulating between Earth's surface and the atmosphere

Selected Bibliography

American Geophysical Union. "Right Mix of Trees Fights Global Warming." *ScienceDaily*. May 1, 2007. http://www.sciencedaily.com/videos/2007/0504-right_mix_of_trees_fights_global_warming.htm (May 14, 2008).

Berger, John J. *Beating the Heat: Why and How We Must Stop Global Warming*. Berkeley, CA: Berkeley Hills Books, 2000.

Bloomberg News. "China Overtakes U.S. in Greenhouse Gas Emissions." *International Herald Tribune*. June 20, 2007. http://www.iht.com/articles/2007/06/20/business/emit.php (May 12, 2008).

Borenstein, Seth. "Spring Keeps Coming Earlier for Birds, Bees, Trees." *USA Today*. March 19, 2008. http://www.usatoday.com/weather/climate/globalwarming/2008-03-19-warming-spring_N.htm (March 21, 2008).

Burgermeister, Jane. "Germany to Require Renewables for New Homes in 2009." *Renewable Energy World.com Online*. December 10, 2007. http://www.renewableenergyworld.net/rea/news/story?id=50746 (May 16, 2008).

Christianson, Gale E. *Greenhouse: The 200-Year Story of Global Warming*. New York: Walker and Company, 1999.

D'Aleo, Joseph. "Global Warming—Is Carbon Dioxide Getting a Bad Rap?" *Energy Tribune*. July 9, 2007. http://www.energytribune.com/articles.cfm?aid=544 (May 13, 2008).

Eilperin, Juliet. "Antarctic Ice Sheet Is Melting Rapidly." *Washington Post*. March 3, 2006. http://www.washingtonpost.com/wp-dyn/content/article/2006/03/02/AR2006030201712.html (May 16, 2008).

"Glacial National Park Is a Global Warming Laboratory." *Sierra Club*. N.d. http://www.sierraclub.org/globalwarming/articles/glacier.asp (May 16, 2008).

Grant, Miles. "Polar Bear Threatened Listing Weakened by Contradictions." *National Wildlife Federation*. May 14, 2008. http://www.nwf.org/news/story.cfm?pageId=E9055F92-F1F6-7B10-3788A03291E5C483 (May 16, 2008).

Grant, Tim, and Gail Littlejohn. *Teaching About Climate Change*. British Columbia, Canada: New Society Publishers, 2001.

"Greenhouse Gases." *CO_2 CRC—Cooperative Research Centre for Greenhouse Gas Technologies.* May 6, 2008. http://www.co2crc.com.au/needgeo/greenhouse_gases.html (May 13, 2008).

Hinsch, Christian. "Sunny Outlook in Saxony: Juwi Installs the World's Biggest Thin-Film Solar Array, Setting a Milestone for Photovoltaic Development." *Renewable Energy Industry.* April 23, 2007. http://www.renewable-energy-industry.com/business/press-releases/newsdetail.php?changeLang=en_GB&newsid=2469 (May 17, 2008).

"Issues: Global Warming: Health." *The Select Committee on Energy Independence and Global Warming.* 2008. http://globalwarming.house.gov/issues/globalwarming?id=0006 (May 15, 2008).

Kanellos, Michael. "Can Baking Soda Curb Global Warming?" *CNET News.com.* November 27, 2007. http://www.news.com/2102-13838_3-6220127.htm (May 13, 2008).

Koerner, Brendan I. "Is Global Warming Caused by Water Vapor?" *Slate.* January 22, 2008. http://www.slate.com/id/2182564/ (May 13, 2008).

Layton, Julia. "What Does Global Warming Have to Do with the Decline in the Polar Bear Population?" *HowStuffWorks.* March 2008. http://science.howstuffworks.com/polar-bear-global-warming.htm (May 16, 2008).

Mok, Kimberley D. "International Team of Scientists to Test South Atlantic Carbon Sink in 2009." September 14, 2007. *Treehugger.com.* http://www.treehugger.com/files/2007/09/international_t.php (May 20, 2008).

National Oceanic and Atmospheric Administration. "Carbon Dioxide, Methane Rise Sharply in 2007." *NOAA.* April 23, 2008. http://www.noaanews.noaa.govstories2008/20080423_methane.html (May 14, 2008).

Oregon State University. "Ice Cores Reveal Fluctuations in Earth's Greenhouse Gases." *ScienceDaily.* May 17, 2008.

http://www.sciencedaily.com/releases/2008/05/080514131131.htm (May 17, 2008).

Pringle, Laurence. *Global Warming*. New York: Seastar Books, 2001.

Revkin, Andrew C. "In a New Climate Model, Short-Term Cooling in a Warmer World." *The New York Times*. May 1, 2008. http://www .nytimes.com/2008/05/01/science/earth/01climate.html?partner =rssnyt&emc=rss (May 14, 2008).

"Rich Countries Gain, Poor Countries Lose Forest Cover." *Mongabay.com*. March 13, 2007. http://news.mongabay.com/2007/0313-forests.html (May 16, 2008).

Schneider, Stephen H. *Laboratory Earth*. New York: Basic Books, 1997.

Science Daily. "First-ever 'State of the Carbon Cycle Report' Finds Troubling Imbalance." *ScienceDaily*. November 17, 2007. http://www .sciencedaily.com/releases/2007/11/071114111141.htm (May 14, 2008).

Society of Chemical Industry. "'Burpless' Grass Cuts Methane Gas from Cattle, May Help Reduce Global Warming." *ScienceDaily*. May 6, 2008. http://www.sciencedaily.com/releases/2008/05/080506120859 .htm (May 14, 2008).

Solomon, Lawrence. "Americans Cooling to Global Warming." *NationalPost*. May 15, 2008. http://network.nationalpost.com/np/ blogs/fpcomment/archive/2008/05/15/solomon.aspx (May 15, 2008).

"10 Ways to Go Green and Save Green." *Worldwatch Institute*. 2007. http://worldwatch.org/node/3915 (May 8, 2008).

U.S. Environmental Protection Agency. "Climate Change: Basic Information." *EPA*. April 1, 2008. http://www.epa.gov/climatechange/ basicinfo.html (May 8, 2008).

Watson, Traci. "States Remove Local Barriers to Eco-Friendly Homes." *USA Today*. May 12, 2008. http://www.usatoday.com/money/ industries/energy/2008-05-12-green_N.htm (May 17, 2008).

West, Larry. "U.S. Autos Account for Half of Global Warming Linked to Cars Worldwide." *About.com: Environmental Issues*. 2007. http:// environment.about.com/od/globalwarming/a/autoemissions.htm (May 13, 2008).

For Further Information

Books:

Brezina, Corona. *Climate Change (In the News)*. New York: Rosen Publishing Group, 2007.

David, Laurie, and Cambria Gorden. *The Down-to-Earth Guide to Global Warming*. London: Orchard Books, 2007.

Gore, Al. *An Inconvenient Truth: The Crisis of Global Warming*. New York: Viking, 2007.

Jefferis, David. *Green Power: Eco-Energy Without Pollution*. New York: Crabtree Publishing Company, 2006.

Johnson, Rebecca. *Investigating Climate Change: Scientists' Search for Answers in a Warming World*. Minneapolis: Twenty-First Century Books, 2009.

Johnson, Rebecca. *Understanding Global Warming*. Minneapolis: Lerner Publications, 2009.

Morris, Neil. *Global Warming (What If We Do Nothing?)*. Milwaukee, WI: World Almanac Library, 2006.

Saunders, Nigel, and Steven Chapman. *Renewable Energy*. Chicago: Raintree, 2005.

Stefoff, Rebecca. *Al Gore: Fighting for a Greener Planet*. Minneapolis: Lerner Publications, 2009.

Tanaka, Shelley. *Climate Change*. Berkeley, CA: Groundwood Books, 2006.

Thornhill, Jan. *This Is My Planet: The Kids' Guide to Global Warming*. Toronto, Ontario: Maple Tree Press, 2007.

Walker, Niki. *Harnessing Power from the Sun*. New York: Crabtree Publishing Company, 2006.

Websites:

The Effects of Global Warming
   http://www.time.com/time/2001/globalwarming/house.html. Check out this interactive activity. Click on parts of a house to see things your family can do to combat global warming.

EPA Global Warming Site
   http://www.epa.gov/globalwarming. Here you can find links to information on the global warming problem, greenhouse gases, what's being done, and what you can do to help.

The EPA Global Warming Kids Site
   http://www.epa.gov/globalwarming/kids. This site has kid-friendly, easy-to-understand information on climate and weather, the greenhouse effect, global warming, how you can make a difference, and links to games and activities relating to global warming.

Nature Challenge for Kids
   http://www.davidsuzuki.org/kids. This site has kid-friendly ways to save energy and help the environment at home, going places, and eating.

NDRC's The Green Squad
   http://www.nrdc.org/greensquad/intro/intro_1.asp. Meet four environmentally conscious students known as the Green Squad, who will help you identify and solve environmental problems. Explore a virtual school where you can try to locate possible environmental problems.

Resource Conservation Challenge Update
   http://www.epa.gov/epaoswer/osw/conserve/resources/rcc-rpt3.pdf. This online pamphlet has ways to conserve energy, and information on various recycling programs.

The Sierra Club Global Warming Campaign
   http://www.sierraclub.org/globalwarming. This site has links to information on the effects of global warming and what you can do to stop it.

Index

Photo Acknowledgments

The images in this book are used with the permission of: The Illustrated London News, p. 5;
© Laura Westlund/Independent Picture Service, pp. 6, 9 (bottom), 14, 22; NASA/JSC, p. 9 (top);
NASA-HQ-GRIN, p. 12; Ron Miller, p. 13; © Bill Hauser/Independent Picture Service,
pp. 16, 32; © age fotostock/SuperStock, pp. 19, 69; © Jacques Jangoux/Alamy, p. 24; Agricultural
Research Service, USDA, p. 26 (top); © Jeff Breedlove/Dreamstime.com/Dreamstime.com, p. 26
(bottom); © Gary Braasch, p. 27; © Roger Braithwaite/Peter Arnold, Inc., p. 31; © Vin Morgan/
AFP/Getty Images, p. 35; © David Harlow/US Geological Survey/Time & Life Pictures/Getty
Images, p. 37 (top); © Philippe Bourseiller/Reportage/Getty Images, p. 37 (bottom); British Crown
Copyright 2005, the Met Office. Illustrated by Laura Westlund/Independent Picture Service, p. 40;
© Paul Andrew Lawrence/drr.net, p. 43; © Mike Sedam/drr.net, p. 44 (top); © Hiroshi Higuchi/
Photographer's Choice/Getty Images, p. 44 (bottom); © Bryan & Cherry Alexander/NHPA/
Photoshot, p. 45; © Yva Momatiuk and John Eastcott/Photo Researchers, Inc., p. 46; Public Affairs
University of British Columbia, p. 48; © Berndt-Joel Gunnarson/Nordic Photos/Getty Images,
p. 51 (bottom); © Stuart Westmorland/Stone/Getty Images, p.51 (top); © Thomas Coex/AFP/
Getty Images, p. 53; © Justin Sullivan/Getty Images, p. 54;© iStockphoto.com/Dan Eckert, p. 55;
© iStockphoto.com/Lev Ezhov, p. 57; AP Photo/Reed Saxon, p. 59; NOAA, p. 60; Jocelyn
Augustino/FEMA, p. 61; © Craig Tuttle/drr.net, p. 62; © iStockphoto.com/Ian Wilson, p. 64;
© Brandon Cole/Visuals Unlimited, p. 66; AP Photo/Eduardo DiBaia, p. 71; © China Photos/
Getty Images, p. 73 (top); © PhotosIndia/Getty Images, p. 73 (bottom); © Jorg Greuel/Digital
Vision/Getty Images, p. 75; © PhotoXpress/ZUMA Press, p. 76; © Romilly Lockyer/The Image
Bank/Getty Images, p. 78; © iStockphoto.com/Richard Schmidt-Zuper, p. 79; © Edward Parker/
Alamy, p. 81; © iStockphoto.com/Volker Kreinacke, p. 82; © Tom Brakefield/SuperStock, p. 83;
© Marcel Mochet/AFP/Getty Images, p. 84; © Images&Stories/Alamy, p. 85; © iStockphoto.com/
Mario Savoia, p. 87; © iStockphoto.com/Jean Schweitzer, p. 89; AP Photo/Kevork Djansezian, p. 93
(top); AP Photo/Steven Senne, p.93 (bottom); © Todd Strand/Independent Picture Service, pp. 94-
95 (right); © Julie Caruso, p. 95 (left); © Julie Caruso/Independent Picture Service, p. 96; © Don
Hammond/Design Pics/drr.net, p. 97; AP Photo/David Zalubowski, p. 99 (top); © Wang Leng/Asia
Images/Getty Images, p. 99 (bottom); © Stuart O'Sullivan/Taxi/Getty Images, p. 100.

Cover: © Colin Monteath/Hedgehog House/Minden Pictures/Getty Images.

About the Authors

Dr. Alvin Silverstein is a former Professor of Biology and Director of the Physician
Assistant Program at the College of Staten Island of the City University of New York.
Virginia B. Silverstein is a translator of Russian scientific literature.

The Silversteins' collaboration began with a biochemical research project at the
University of Pennsylvania. Since then they have produced six children and more than
two hundred published books that have received high acclaim for their clear, timely, and
authoritative coverage of science and health topics.

Laura Silverstein Nunn, a graduate of Kean College, began helping with the research for
her parents' books while she was in high school. Since joining the writing team, she has
coauthored more than eighty books.